The Fascinating World of Poems

Poorvi Rajak

Anuragyam, New Delhi

© Poorvi Rajak

This book has been published with all reasonable efforts taken to make the material error-free after the consent of the author. No part of this book shall be used, reproduced in any manner whatsoever without written permission from the author, except in the case of brief quotations embodied in critical articles and reviews.

The Author of this book is solely responsible and liable for its content including but not limited to the views, representations, descriptions, statements, information, opinions and references ["Content"]. The Content of this book shall not constitute or be construed or deemed to reflect the opinion or expression of the Publisher or Editor. Neither the Publisher nor Editor endorse or approve the Content of this book or guarantee the reliability, accuracy or completeness of the Content published herein and do not make any representations or warranties of any kind, express or implied, including but not limited to the implied warranties of merchantability, fitness for a particular purpose. The Publisher and Editor shall not be liable whatsoever for any errors, omissions, whether such errors or omissions result from negligence, accident, or any other cause or claims for loss or damages of any kind, including without limitation, indirect or consequential loss or damage arising out of use, inability to use, or about the reliability, accuracy or sufficiency of the information contained in this book.

Publication by
Anuragyam, New Delhi
www.anuragyam.com
editor@anuragyamgmail.com
+91-9999920037

Cover Design:
Er. Sachin Chaturvedi, Anuragyam

Illustration:
Poorvi Rajak (Child Artist & Author)

Printing & Marketing by: Notion Press
Distribution: Anuragyam, Notion Press, Amazon, Flipkart

I dedicate this little book

to our Nation

Velagapudi Ramakrishna Babu
MLA

Visakhapatnam East Constituency
Visakhapatnam

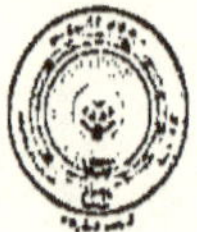

Phone : 0891- 2799999
Mobile : 9393120999
Fax   : 0891-2791999

Date:29-12-2022
Visakhapatnam

I am Velagapudi Ramakrishna Babu, a Member of Legislative Assembly at Visakhapatnam East Constituency. The author Poorvi Rajak, is a young and dynamic student. I have been observing her since she was three. She is a multitasking girl. Apart from writing poems, she is excellent in many activities like Drawing, Painting, story writing & telling, karate, public speaking, social work, to name it a few. She also raises awareness about the degrading condition of the environment and she also encourages her friends to plant trees.

She also organises beach cleanup programmes. She is one of the shining stars in the city and has won numerous awards in many competitions at national, international, state , district and city level. I am still amazed by how she is able to pen such arousing poems at such a tender age.

I'm sure she is going to make a difference in the society by her inspiring words. I congratulate her on publishing her first book of poems.

Thanking You,

Yours Sincerely

(Velagapudi Ramakrishna Babu)

Name: Purvi Rajak D/o Sunil Rajak
Address:Lig-38,Sector-1,MVP Colony,
1st Floor,Visakhapatnam
Mob:9553668255
Mamtarajak1984@gmail.com

Innovators of Quality Education since 1983

Affiliated to CBSE New Delhi
Affiliation No. : 130196

Date: 24.12.2022

MESSAGE

Poorvi Rajak, has been studying in Little Angels School right from LKG and currently she is in Class 7. As the Founder & Chairman of Little Angels School, I know her very intimately since the beginning and have seen her progress over the years.

She is a very promising and a focused student. She is confident, committed, straightforward and meticulous in her works. She is an all-rounder in all aspects and has a multifaceted vision. She is very passionate about pursuing extracurricular activities along with academics and makes efforts to develop her artistic skills and create something new. She is always supported and encouraged by her school and teachers in every walk of her life.

She never ceases from taking part in competitions and winning prizes and awards. She is a name to reckon in the city of Visakhapatnam when it comes to painting and elocution competitions. Poorvi's name is also featured in the India Book of Records for her innovative artwork of representing the map of India using seashells. She has created a record for using "Maximum seashells painted with different art forms of all Indian States". She painted 286 seashells with different art forms of all 28 Indian States. She has achieved this feat on 23rd August, 2022.

Her ambition is to become an IAS officer and work for the development of the country. She primarily wants to contribute towards the development of education for girl child. Her parents Mr. Sunil Rajak and Mrs. Mamta Rajak always support and encourage her to explore new avenues and challenges. Her latest work is a compilation of 75 poems through which she has expressed her thoughts on various topics ranging from her love for her mother, vision for India, Nature and Environment, Social causes and many others. Her maiden effort is noteworthy and deserves to be appreciated.

I heartily congratulate her and on behalf of entire Little Angels Family wish her all the best for future endeavours.

M. Venumonan
Founder & Chairman
Little Angels School, Visakhapatnam

Sector-3, MVP Colony, Visakhapatnam- 530017, Andhra Pradesh, India. Ph: 0891-2553221
Email : littleangelschoolsvizag@yahoo.co.in | Website : www.littleangels.org.in

Forewords

When I was asked to write a foreword for the author of this Poetry Book collection, I was surprised by this young vibrant and talented young lady. She is only 11 years old and in grade 7 but has already achieved so much and is truly inspirational for the old and young.

Firstly, I would like to congratulate Poorvi Rajak for being an inspiration to all of us, you truly captured my heart. Poorvi is an Author, Artist, Public Speaker, and Karateka. She is an awardee of the Indian Book of Records and a Gold Medallist.

As a confident, committed, straightforward young lady and very meticulous in her work, she proves to be focused as an all-rounder in all aspects and has a multifaceted vision she is very passionate about pursuing extracurricular activities and exceptional academic student who makes effort to develop her artistic skills and always open minded to try something new.

As an extraordinary student, she has the full support of her teachers, parents, and peers who encourage her to reach her full potential and fulfil her dreams. She does not shy away from taking part in competitions and seizes every opportunity to do her best and always tries to win prizes and awards.

She is a force to reckon with in her city, Visakhapatnam when it comes to painting and elocution competitions.

Although she accomplished already so much at a young age Poorvi stays humble and encourages everyone else to reach for their dreams and never to give up.

Her book consists of 75 poems in which she wrote about nature, patriotism, and love for animals, politics, imagination, women's rights, coronavirus, education, and sweets. In conclusion, I like to encourage every reader to be like Poorvi Rajak, never to give up and always reach for the stars.

Keep on shining Poorvi, love you always.

Roebain Christians
International Author, Poetess & Educator
Cape Town, Western Cape, South Africa
Email: roebainchristians6@gmail.com

Introduction

This book is a collection of what is my favourite hobby – writing poems. I began writing poems at the age of 10.Well, I am 11 now (as of 2022).I started writing poems when we got an assignment to write a poem on nature. I tried to write a poem which everyone praised. My parents encouraged me to write more poems and I have written around a 100 poems in the past year. I realized that 75 years have passed since Independence and decided to bring out a book of 75 poems, each for a year of Independence.

Some of the poems like Love for India express my love for the country and some like Save Ozone and Soil Erosion – The Erosion of the Earth aim to highlight the problems faced by nature due to human activities. Few of the poems like Never Lose Hope are about the thoughts I have, The World OF Cream and Arrogant Corona are a product of my imagination, and Jhansi Ki Rani and Mitali Madhumita are about the brave women of India... The list is endless .Each Poem in this book is from the core of my heart and there is a story about how each poem is written.

Poorvi Rajak

Acknowledgments

First of all I would like to thank my parents from the bottom of my heart. They are like my backbone and always support me.

My heartfelt thanks to the founder of Anuragyam, Mr. Sachin Chaturvedi for supporting me a lot in everything. Without his help I would not have been able to get the book published.

My hearty thanks to the Founder and Chairman of our school, Mr. M. Venu Mohan for writing the preface. Last but not the least my warm thanks to all my teachers.

Poorvi Rajak

**Dr. Yatindra Mahobe, Realistic Artist, Head, Department of Drawing and Painting
Govt. S. S. N. M. Mahila Mahavidyalaya. Narsinghpur, Madhya Pradesh, India**

Poems

Greatness of My Mother

You are the greatest force in the world
Thanks to you I am ever pearled
You are the blue rose in the sea of red ones
With you every place feels like the heavens

Dearest Mumma, you are my backbone,
You help me to accomplish every goal
You are the colourful rose that brightens my world
And the rare gems which are fabled

You are the most compassionate person
Who inculcated every strength into me with passion
I will love you till the mountains and seas exist
With the toughest difficulties you persist

I thank you from the bottom of my heart for everything
And the love which is truly everlasting
I am forever indebted for love which is pure
With this, I thank for the greatest gift I received from nature

Marvelous Nature

Look at these trees
They give us cool breeze
May they never cease
To shelter beautiful bees

Look at this river
With water of sparkling silver
It holds lovely gems
Of fish and plants of lovely stems

Look at the lovely sky
With clouds so high
With birds of every colour
Chirping in chorus

May these never perish
For us to cherish
With birds and fish
They will never cease

The Author is very creative in such a small age. She is very fluent in the art of handling language. She is such a perfectionist and fine tunes her ideas to give the readers the best.

K M Dinesh Babu
Scientist / Engineer - SF
Department of Space, Indian Space Research Organisation
Satish Dhawan Space Centre, Sriharikota, Andhra Pradesh

Poorvi Rajak is one of the brightest students of Little Angels School, Visakhapatnam. Apart from being excellent in her academics, she is a multi-talented child with excellent Oratory skills. She has good hands in Art and Craft and is always creative in her work. She takes pride in taking the lead in all school activities and has always brought laurels to the school. She has a great passion for writing and is very spontaneous in penning down her thoughts. All her works are creative and unique always. Her enthusiasm and achievements makes her a source of inspiration for her peer group. My hearty congratulations to Poorvi on the launch of her book. Wishing her success in all her future endeavors. All the Best!!

Mrs. Indu Malini N.
Vice Principal
Little Angels School, MVP Branch, VSP

Wonderful Science

Science is always revered everywhere
It contributed a lot to agriculture and healthcare
Life is impossible without the discoveries made by science
It helps to develop the world, body and mind

Science is equal to god in his heavenly abode
Confusing things it helps to decode
Science is the understanding of this world
And has had it ever pearled

We would be lost without science
It gives us useful information of the smallest things,
including rice
We are thankful for this gift to mankind
And there will be no better gift of this kind

Poorvi is a very disciplined and well-mannered child. She is an enthusiastic learner. Moreover, she is very good at listening, reading, writing and speaking as well. Her communication skills were excellent that's why she was selected as an Anchor for the KG Day. She is regular to school and received 100% attendance award. She is very friendly with the peer group. She was an active participant in all the class activities and was a winner in most of the Competitions held in the academic year. Being her LKG teacher, I can say that she was an all-rounder at that tender age. She wishes all her teachers on every Teachers Day every year with a beautiful handmade greeting card which shows her respect towards teachers. She is an amazing student. I'm proud to be a Kindergarten Teacher (LKG) to such a multi-faceted child. Wishing her success in her future   endeavors.

Mrs. R Hemalatha
Class counsellor LKG – 2014-2015

Poorvi was academically excellent, well-behaved, very good story teller, helpful to others, active participant in all activities.

Mrs. Manjula
Class counsellor I – 2016-2017

Mother Earth

Mother Earth was green and fresh
But now she is in a mess
Because of increasing pollution
We need to take precaution

Save natural resources with all your might
Otherwise we will be out of sight
Don't take it mildly
Otherwise we will all run wildly

Save everything you can now
Otherwise you will mourn
The earth will become a useless ball
And will be abandoned by all

My Vision of India

My vision of India in 100 years is a promising India
In which we all will still follow our golden culture
as proud Indians
We will retrieve the Kohinoor and Peacock throne
of the Mughals
And be able to do all sorts of things, like travelling
in giant bubbles!

Huge schools, hospitals and shops will pop out
in small villages
There will be no corruption; poverty or harshness,
there will be truthfulness
Agriculture will increase in leaps and bounds,
so will the forest cover,
Corona and it's siblings will vanish, of diseases
there will be no danger

People will develop and yet take care of nature
and make it more beautiful
They will make many mouth dropping inventions
and be dutiful
Scientists will discover many more interesting
theories and facts
There will be factories without the hazardous impacts

Animals will be able to talk like humans
And we will be best friends

The bond of animal human relationship deeper
and deeper will extend
Poaching will be a thing of the past, animals will forever last
The future world will develop so quickly and fast

I would like to tell even more about my vision
In which India becomes the champion
I would like to end my description here
And tell you all about it later

I Salute the Fallen Heroes of India

I salute the fallen heroes of India
Who gave the light of freedom to all Indians
Who suffered under the onslaught of British
The freedom fighters of India left us undiminished

Never forget Chandrasekhar Azad, Rani Lakshmi Bai,
Bhagat Singh, Alluri Sitarama Raju, Lala Lajpat Rai
And many uncountable fallen heroes who fought for our
independence
And all those who removed us from dependence

Remember Bal Gangadhar Tilak who fought for our rights
And Mahatma Gandhi who fought for our plight
Also Sarojini Naidu the great Indian poet
Who fought against the British till her end

These people will never cease from the hearts of the people
For they led us out of trouble
We salute their noble deeds
For they fought for our needs

For the people of India they fought
Our independence they brought
Every rule of the British they disagreed
That's why we are all free

Save Elephants

Look at the majestic elephant
With its look so elegant
It is the royal ride
Our nation's pride

They were the vehicles of the kings
As they went around the mills
How much they were treasured!
Their worth was never measured

But look at the condition they are in now
They have lost their royal crown
They are endangered
We must be their savior

Merciless humans hunted them for their tusks
For them ivory of elephant is precious
Than elephants
We must save these lovely gems

Millions of elephants could be saved
If we stopped this unkind trade
We must take this vow
That we will save elephants from now

IT WOULD BE GREAT IF HUMANS TOOK GOOD CARE OF US !
YES!

My Feelings about Poetry

Poetry is a wonderful thing to express our feelings
The joy, agony, excitement and pleadings
For the needy people and the helpless animals
And against the unjust rules and taxes set by the politicians

Poetry is a thing with which we trust our thoughts
Secrets, fears, likes and naughts
Of course the pen is mightier than the sword
Poetry is a thing about the unexplored

Poetry is a tool through we speak for or against anything
Poetry is a tool through which many think
Through poetry we can change the world
The depth of poetry is never measured

Poetry is a shining silk cloth
Which cannot be destroyed by any moth
To me writing poetry is a part of my life
A thing which cannot be cut by any knife

My Soul Mates

My soul mates are my parents
When I am tired they are my refreshments
In my moments of confusion they are my guides
In my heart they forever reside

The most unique ideas they suggest
They are forever my soul mates
They trust me, I trust them
They are my stem; I am the branches on them

My parents are my soul mates
They are everywhere
They help me mend my fears
We have an inseparable bond over the years

Parents are my pride
Because they give me life
I always have faith in them
My parents are forever my soul mates

True Love

A true love is hard to find
Because they should be our mentor and side
Crush starts from the eyes
Dining and roaming side to side
Eternal love is from the heart
For the mental state of love is pure and always starts
Great lovers like Romeo and Juliet
Have set the many lover's of the world mindset
It never starts and never ends
Jolly lover's hearts easily mends
Kind lovers help each other
Love is just like a mother
Merciful lovers never die
Never cease as they pass by
On the lips of bliss they rest
Pure lovers are always the best
Questioning each other time to time
Rays of sun falling on them as they are side by side
Singing forever melodious songs
The songs worth infinite pounds
Ultimate lovers never complain
Virtuous lovers are each other's soulmate
Wherever they are love is always there
Xylophone music they play for each other
You are my true love they sing to each other
Zigzag lines never poses problems for true lovers,
for their love is immortal

Friendship

Friendship is a treasure which money cannot buy
In the most difficult situations they keep our hopes high
Friends always dye our lives
They are ever kind

Friends push you to be the best
The best ideas they suggest
Friends improve the quality of life
They are always our side

Friendship fills our lives with meaning
Their words are appealing
Friends dream together
Friendship lives forever

Friendship is a treasure which withstands destruction
Friendship is all about protection
Friends are always sane
Without friends our lives would never be the same

The Fascinating World of Poems

Poorvi Rajak is an expressive child, fearless and independent. She is courteous and responsible, meticulous and organized in her work. Moreover she is observant and always willing to learn. She has originality in her thoughts. Furthermore she is friendly and always willing to help others. Apart from academics she used to show keen interest in drawing and craft work. She joined social studies club in class 2 and continued in the same club for three consecutive years. It was a joyful experience teaching her.

Mrs. K. Aparna
Class counsellor II – 2017-2018

It's a great privilege to share a few words about such a cute, pro-active, hard-working, lovely Little Angel, my favorite student Poorvi Rajak. The secret of getting ahead is getting started. So, all her dreams are coming true with her continuous hard work, leadership quality, determination and her courage to pursue them. Smart people like Poorvi can learn anything from everything and everyone. The word "Impossible" is not found in her dictionary. Magic is there in her words. She holds her vision, trusts the process to reach her goal. She has the ability to write good poems in an artistic form as she is a good artist, good at extempore, good anchor for many events in the school and out of campus also. She can encourage and change people's minds with her mesmerizing words. She addresses public problems and tries to give solutions through her poems, paintings and drawings. She is honored with many prestigious rewards and awards. Frankly speaking, she is an All-rounder. She is the best example for overall development. I congratulate her for her great work on different issues and bringing them to us by publishing them in the form a book. I wish her that she gets many more laurels in her future and continues the legacy.

Mrs. Lalita Pantula
Class counsellor IV - 2019- 2020

Injustice to Women

A woman is the queen of the world
Who is ever pearled
A woman is everything
A woman is like a bird who is always singing

Despite of all this
Many women face problems
Many face discrimination
Many miss their education

Many are victims of child marriage
Women are always discouraged
Made to do household chores
As all her dreams are poured

Oh what is all this cruelty?
In spite of all her jewellery
Women must raise their voice
They should be treated equally with boys

Women are no lesser than boys
Yet the women do work and boys enjoy!
Women and men must be treated equally
Only then the world will live peacefully

The Magical Forest

I walk through the silent forest
Collecting fruits the choicest
Then the bees flutter around me
Giving me the sweetest honey

Walking alone with the honey
The birds flutter around me
Their lovely feathers I see
And choicest mangoes they give from the forestry

Searching for water around the forest
A turtle gave me a glass strongest
As I touched the glass
A pool of water comes through the grass

As I wandered around in the cold
A lion came with a sweater, around me it rolled
It took me to its den
And gave a me fantabulous pen

This is the beauty of nature
Filled with animals, their kindness is greater
Our future nature nurtures
We must take care of nature

My Favourite Animals

Armadillo, an armoured animal, its armour cosy
Bee, the animal that gives us delicious honey
Cat, the cute and friendly tiger
Dog our adorable sider
Eagle the majestic bird
Flamingo the one leg sleeper, the quality it deserves
Gorillas the relatives of humans
Hare the cutest animal, its surrounding it illumines
Immortal jellyfish the animal which is immortal
Jackabee dog, our supporter
Kangaroos the heavyweight high jumpers
Lioness, the majestic runner
Macaw the king of the birds, my most favorite bird
Nightingale, whose singing is never gone unheard
Opossum the cute teddy bear like animal, playing possum
Puffin the bird whose colourful beak is just like blossom
Quetzal a bird with a long tail
Reindeer the animal which pulls Santa's sleigh
Seahorse the horse of the sea
Turtle the long lived animal, it will always be
Umbrella bird the umbrella headed bird
Vulture the scavenger, the cleanup crew is never deterred
White tiger the snowy furry animal
X-Ray Tetra striped fin fish, is never a cannibal
Yak the furry mountain beast
Zebra the striped animal, on green grass it feeds

Caution to the Birds

I love birds, I say to the macaw
Especially you I gaze in awe!
As I say this all the birds come around me
I say, dear crow, your glossy feathers are lovely

O beautiful myhna your beak is as bright as the sun
You look cute when you dance in the rain for fun
Graceful teetar, your nest is as beautiful as you
Sitting on a branch, you are of great value

Magpie, you Feathers are soft as snow
Your song is forever mellow
O charming dove, you are a symbol of peace
I name you snow white, the white bird dancing in the breeze

O colourful and graceful birds
I warn that you are in a great hazard
Humans mercilessly hunt you down
Be careful if you don't want to mourn

They cage you in tiny cages
In which you will be caught for ages
I wish humans don't hunt birds, just wish for their welfare
To this the birds said, then we will all prepare for a fanfare

Stop Child Labour

A child thin and weak, is at a garbage dump
Collecting wood, paper and plastic lumps
All the while thinking of education
His world is in isolation

Millions of children are in child labour
Tonnes of bricks on their backs they bear
They are made to build buildings and schools
But not live or study in them, they are made to hold tools

The future of the world rests on children
But they are engaged in labour, their future hidden
Many children remain illiterate
So the future of the world is the bitterest

Education is every child's birthright
They should be relived from their plight
Send them to school
So that they become jewels

Children should be educated
To the world they will be dedicated
The world will brighten forever
And live together forever

Gorgeous Flowers

Filled with beauty and fragrance, beautiful rose
You must be the queen of flowers I suppose
You must be the lovely red portion of a garland
Which is going to be presented to god who is radiant

O Beautiful daisy, bright and huge
All types of colours for your flowers you choose
Where do you get those lovely colours from
I think you make those colours custom

O beautiful hibiscus, graceful and soft
Your beauty fills love in the heart
From where do you get your shape of lovely petals ?
Maybe the supreme personality in you it dwells

These lovely flowers together form a posy
The beauty of the posy is a fantasy
I wish people would take care of flowers
Otherwise they will be photos printed on a tower

Request for the Animals

To whom does the whole earth belong to?
Most of you think it belongs to humans, true?
Who has the right to eat the fruits of the trees?
Hope so the answer is not humans, please

The earth belongs to the universe
Which has many creatures numerous
All living things have the right to eat the fruits
The sound of the beings is melodious like of a flute

Humans have stolen the earth from the universe
Whose beauty is diverse
Have chopped down trees mercilessly
And built cities sumptuously

Many animals lay down never to rise again
But for humans a new era has begun
My humble request to everyone is to plant trees
Atleast one, if you can, please?

A new life will begin for animals
And they will reside in their own capitals
The earth will return back to normal
And all living creatures will live happily forever

Selfless Ocean

The ocean is the base of the world
Precious gems and creatures it holds
Oceans always help us in times of need
It never thinks about greed

But sometimes it goes wild
And flings things aside
Because it is so disappointed with humans
Yet it gives humans gems

Do you know the reason why it goes wild on humans?
Humans overfish and disrupt its balance!
Carelessly throw trash into the ocean
And the creatures inside throw up a commotion

The Ocean goes wild on the pacific dump on her
And then she gives her signal of danger
The ocean easily gives us life without expectations
And can take it away without any demonstrations

Love for India

We are the pride of India
We are her lovely bindiya
No one can stop us from doing what we like
We are forever undivided, we are always alike

Our determination knows no bounds, it has no end
Whenever India is in danger, her pride we always defend
India can never be snatched from us, No one can
steal her pride
No one will steal her until we are alive, until we
are at her side

India is not a mere country, she is the biggest continent
We will fight for India, we will become her monument
India is the universe to us, she is our life
She is our pride, she is our guide

India is a shining star, India is the sun
We are India's armour, the battle against the British we won
India is the mother of many great leaders
India is so diverse, no one has her features

We are the backbone of India, we are her guards
We will fight for India until we are shards
Look at India's lovely crown the great Himalayas
We will always save her, if she is in crisis

I don't care if I am dead, but India should be unscathed
India's beauty and pride no one can match
Until we are alive she will be in peace
How much anyone tries to steal her, she will never cease

Corrupt Politicians

Down with the corrupt politicians
Helpless people they churn
Their promises are just white lies
And then the state or country has to pay the price

Down with their fake welfare brouchers
All the perfect rules they alter
They pay bribes to win elections and awards
The only ones that can save us from their tyranny are the gods

The corrupt politicians just enjoy their lifestyle
And the good people have to pay the price
We can all snatch their power away as easily we gave them
And bring back the real rulers who are the real gems

Priceless Wisdom

Wisdom is a thing which is rare
It makes sure the world is never bare
It is a thing which few possess
It never fails to lead us to success

Wisdom is from the mind
Our lost treasure it helps us to find
Wisdom can never be handed down in books
Sometimes it is inaccessible even to dukes

Wisdom cannot be compared to wealth
It always saves our health
Wisdom always saves the world
Many generations it has fabled

Always be careful with wisdom
Because sometimes it will make you blossom
And if it is not used properly
It will surely be deadly

Use wisdom with wisdom
And you will have a kingdom
And you will live happily
And everyone will be jolly

Importance of Teachers

I bow to the teachers; they shape the future of the world
They think of us, our future they unbuckle
Innumerable sacrifices they make for our welfare
Just imagine how they beared our tantrums,
Noise and stubbornness

Teachers play a very important part in our lives
They enrich our lives and remove all our fears
Without teachers we would always be incomplete
They teach us with unending patience,
their words are ever sweet

The worth of teachers cannot be compared to a precious
diamond
The lamp of courage and aim in us they have lightened
Teachers are the backbone of the world
With the pearls of education the whole world they have
pearled

Teachers play an extremely important role in our lives
Without teachers it is impossible to survive
The future of the world they suggest
To them I offer my utmost respects

The Most Precious Of All

Teachers are very precious in our life
In the most difficult situations they are our side
Teachers are the epitome of our success
They take us out of our nutshells

Teachers educate us without thinking about themselves
They tell us the magic spell
The magic spell of education
They give us precious information

The heart of teachers are always pure
They teach us with their soul
Teachers help us to achieve our goals
Our future they unroll

Just imagine the world without teachers
There would be no doctors, politicians and engineers
We must bow before them
And give them our utmost respect

A teacher is just like a God
Teachers educate us so that we are not odd
Teachers sacrifice their lives for our future
So we must always look up to teachers

The Fascinating World of Poems

"Good Students Aim for Good Grades, But Great Students Aim for Great Goals". It's my privilege to share my views about one of my favorite student Poorvi. Poorvi is very creative in her work and excellent Artist too. She participated in innumerable painting competitions and secured many prizes. She is very organized, hardworking and well planned in all her works. She accepts the challenges with great enthusiasm and completes the task. Even though the year 2020- 21 was conducted in online mode, she participated in many activities virtually. She also took part in planting campaign for Anuragyam, New Delhi & encouraged many students to plant a tree for ecofriendly environment. She is the best example for holistic development. I congratulate her on her tremendous work in composing a book of poems. Wishing her lots of Luck.

Ch. Shakina Petilla
Class Counsellor V - 2020-21

I was extremely impressed by Poorvi's poetry and the thought and emotion she puts into each piece. If you are looking for something truly moving and impactful, I would highly recommend reading her poems. I would like to offer my warmest congratulations to the young poet on the publication of her collection of poetry. It is clear that she has a flair for language and a deep understanding of human experience, and I have no doubt that she will continue to produce powerful and evocative works in the future.

Mrs. Reena Mohanto
Class Counsellor VI A - 2021-22

The Quiz

I woke up early in the morning
My thoughts were soaring
I had a quiz that day
And I was not well prepared, I say

I went to the school
Gathering knowledge a pool
I rushed to the school auditorium
To find the quiz was about to start

There were four teams, red, yellow, green, blue
I was in red team, my excitement till the sky it flew
Yellow was in a draw with red
Another question will be asked, teacher said

The question was asked
The answer I gave, red passed !
Red won the day
And I returned to the class in abandon gay

The Tough Ways of the World

There is something cheerful today
And with happiness my whole body sways
A dream has come true now
And I can tell you how

After spending hours attending online classes
near the computer
Due to Corona, cooped up in fear
The real world before Covid, at the time was just a dream
And the worries and normal world desires were an
overflowing stream

The stream almost drowned all of us
And day by day the situation became worse
Then one day a ray of light appeared
And ate everything we feared

It drank up the stream of worries
And gave us the cheerful breeze
Everything is returning to normal
And we are living and will live happily forever

The Best Diet

Eat healthy food
And improve your mood
Add eggs to your diet
And against all diseases you will fight
Eat meat, drink milk
And all around you will flit
Eat lots of fruits and veggies
And lots of juicy berries
Eat healthy live healthy
Is the key to be wealthy

The Birds of Peace

O white dove, the messenger of peace
The peace in the world, you make sure it never cease
Carrying the olive branch you fly across the sky
You show the peace's might

O pigeon the ancient messenger
For the senders of letters you were auspicious
You helped many righteous kings in their battle
When their hopes used to shatter

These beauties were taken care of
But now by poachers they are shot
Mercilessly shot for their meat
While they were flying in the sleet

The Fearless Crow

In my balcony came a crow with one leg
It sat and caw caw it said
It never flew until I gave it a piece of bread
But on one condition, the piece of bread should be wet

Soon it began to bring its friend along
And used to sing the crow song
They had their mega breakfast
They never flew on seeing me, they were the boldest

After a while it bought its friend along
And sang the crow song
Had their brunch
And had their special lunch

Soon the whole family came along
Of my delicious bread they were fond
Keep the bread pieces in a line
And they would seize them in a line

I named them bhukkad and bhukkdi
They are my hungry buddy
They are a happy united crow family
And on bread they feast happily

Never Lose Hope

Never lose hope, no matter what
Even if you lose everything you have a lot
If you are in front of a demon
Your courage you should never shun

Every person owns a star
You just find yours and make your mark
If you want to shine like the sun
Then you have to burn under the sun

Achieve what you want with fun
But never against anyone use a gun
Live the way you want to live
But any one's luck you must never deprive

Go ahead and be a good human being
And everyone about you they will sing
Just search your own talent
Go ahead and become gallant

Unique Forests

Forests are the pride of the world
The greenery of the world they have unfurled
They shelter flocks of birds and precious animals
And beautiful creepers and chrysan the mums

Merciless humans are cutting the forests
Acers and acres of them they deforest
Many exotic plants and animals have disappeared
Making our lives weird

Many great souls like Amrita devi saved trees
They offered their lives to save trees
Save trees, promote afforestation
About saving trees give education

Without trees the world will see its end
Because on trees the world depends
Save trees save forests
And the earth will become gorgeous

I recently had the opportunity to read a collection of poetry by young writer Poorvi Rajak, and I was positively impressed by the depth and emotion contained within the pieces. The use of language is masterful, and each poem seemed to strike a chord within me, evoking a range of emotions from joy to sadness to contemplation. I wish the young poet all the best in her future endeavors, and hope that she continue to share her insights and emotions with the world through her poetry. I have no doubt that she will touch the hearts and minds of many readers with her words. Keep up the great work!

Mr. D. Mohanto
Class Counselor VII A - 2022- 23

"From small beginnings come great things." Poorvi is really apt for the above saying as she is incredibly proficient at writing great contextual and thematic poems. On this occasion, I wish Poorvi all the very best in all her endeavors.

Mr. B. Suresh
English Teacher
Little Angels School, MVP Branch, VSP

My Fitness Mantra

My Fitness mantra for a healthy life
Is going to be one of my best guide
First we must always be happy
Then it's exercise which is always pretty
Next is a balanced diet and is always tempting
After that is plenty of water and it's never ending
Always remember to wash hands frequently
Lastly keep your home tidy and heavenly
The is my fitness mantra with which I survive
By just following it, healthily we will thrive

Be Dutiful

Live if you must
But don't forget to be just
Make the whole would beautiful
And always be dutiful

Give everyone precious education
And they will make a beautiful nation
A nation without any poachers
A nation without any tears

A nation full of trees
Which will give us lovely breeze
A nation full of birds
Whose beauty can never be described in words

A nation full of cleanliness
A nation without selfishness
A nation full of kindness
A nation without blindness

A nation whose beauty will spread far and wide
And will always be at our side
It will be the epitome of peace
And will never cease

Let's Unite

Birds migrating in sky
Show the unity's might
Let's unite forever together let's fight
To kindness, let's show the unity's might

Don't waste your money on dress of gold
Burst out of your shells, be bold
Fight against corruption
Let our sprit be a great eruption

Let's change the world
Let's Have it pearled
Come together work together
And live in peace forever

Change the World

We are humans not animals
Yet we behave like cannibals
We must take care of the world
And have it pearled

With the pearls of education it is possible
Nothing is ever impossible
Have the hope and courage to do it
And achieve your aim bit by bit

The world's future is around us
Take care otherwise it will vanish in a gust
You will never be able to find it
Not even a single little bit

The future is on our shoulders
Make your shoulders as strong as boulders
Take care of everything around you
People like you are very few

Change the world with your courage
Your name will be in the divine page
Change it with your wit
And you will change every single bit

Flying Virtuousness

O virtuousness please come flying to us
Riding the wind as your bus
Please help us in this corrupt world
Like milk we are being churned

The government is not helping us
They make us pay taxes, they are not just
They do nothing for us
90% of them are just corrupt

O virtuousness you are our hope
In these difficult times help us to cope
Make the world a better place
Just and full of grace

Let's Shellabrate!

There are some cute creatures underwater
Waggling its beautiful flippers taking it further and further
It has the beautiful shade of green and brown
It is perfect for the cutest creature crown

I am talking about none other than turtles
Overcoming every obstacle
From the mass extinction from the asteroid centuries ago
To the humans polluting the waters, making it yellow and
yellow

Sadly, turtles are in danger
With the plastic of humans polluting their waters
We need to stop polluting their place
And should embrace them with grace

They are poached mercilessly for their meat and shells
And this the mercilessness of humans, clearly it tells
Please spare the innocent turtles
And free them from the inhumane shackles

90 percent of turtles eat plastic and trash
And that plastic makes turtles mash
The turtle's heaven has become hell
And that is the warning bell

Let's shellabrate these lovely creatures
Otherwise they will be just sculptures
Love, share and care for the turtles
In this mission, don't be a hurdle

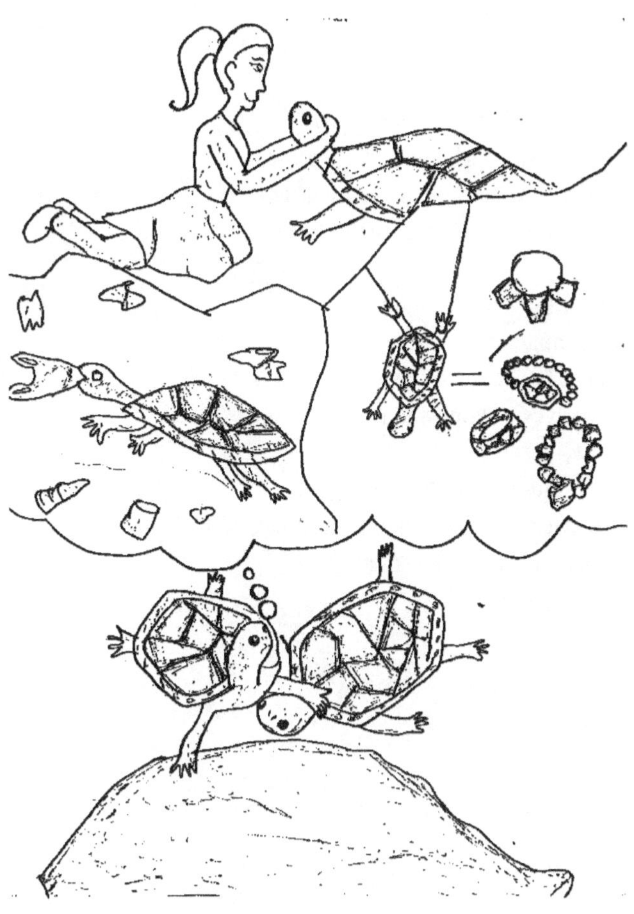

Curious Questions

I wonder how the fruits stay on the trees
Which dance wildly in the breeze ?
I wonder how does the earth hold our weight ?
From millions of years, it never breaks !

I wonder how do the plants grow ?
They suddenly spring out like a brow !
I wonder how the flowers get their colors ?
I wonder how they never break from our fingers ?

I wonder how people think ?
Lovely things they bring !
I wonder how stars shine ?
Which gives us hope and might

How do these things happen how ?
The answer to these someone must have found !
One day we will find a solution
And make a revolution

The City of Destiny

My beautiful Vizag, I love you
Cities like you are rare and few
The west side of you has green mountains
And Kailashgiri hills with beautiful fountains

The east side of you faces the endless sea
Where everyone feels free
You are full of lovely parks and trees
There is not a place in you without a tree

Your beaches in you are fantastic
Truthfully I say you are gigantic
O the city of destiny
The places in you are fancy

O the jewel of the east coast
About your beauty everyone boasts
You will have a place in everyone's hearts
So will your green hills and shipyards

Vizag will never cease from the world
In you everyone is glad
O cosmopolitan city
Always you will have your beauty

The Caring Crow

A crow came crying to me
And said, look at the destruction, see !
My home is going to be devastated
And my friend parrots to be massacred !

Please save the lives of my friends
I don't know what do the people intend !
I said to my friends, save the birds lives
Promise me you will be at their side !

We went to the place and saw the birds crying
And huge logs of wood burning
I asked what happened,
They said suddenly our lives are dampened !

Humans are the demons of this age
The lives of beautiful creatures please spare !
Your carelessness will make the earth bare
Don't kill them even if you dare !

Jhansi Ki Rani

O Jhansi's lioness
You were the finest
You sacrificed your life
For the country you strive

O, Jhansi ki Rani, Rani Lakshmi Bai
You were always kind and wise
With bravery you fought against the British
You made sure that the pride of India is undiminished

You are the incarnation of goddess Durga
You were the ever powerful and clever
We will always remember your sacrifice
Your glory will forever reach the skies

The World of Cream

One day I had a Beautiful Dream
In which I saw A world filled with cream!
Soon the cream turned into things and Shapes
From turtles to Clouds and Rivers to grapes !

Soon it turned in a captivating world
Where anyone could walk into the underworld!
The gods and goddesses visited the world everyday
There were pots of cream and not of clay!

Rives of edible gems and not of water
Where Babies didn't need mothers or fathers!
I pinched myself, and found myself in this magical world
Where even animals by gods were pearled!

Humans that hugged all the shy birds and animals
And even for pinching animals people were
regarded criminals!
There was nothing such as guns, knives or weapons
The world was green and fresh, though inhabited by millions!

Sadly, I woke up to the morning sunshine and vanished
from my dream
And saw a man shooting pigeons with a camera,
my happiness was extreme!
And a cute infant and girl petting a tiger and a woman
kissing a macaw
Sadly, from this dream also I had to withdraw!

Then I really woke up and remembered I had to go to school
And this dream was really millions, trillions worth of
invaluable jewel!
Let's all of us pray to make my dream come true
And everyone immerse themselves in what is new

Save Ozone

The ozone layer of the earth
Is the earth's s only shirt
The ozone layer depletion we have brought
Without thinking of what it costs

The result is global warming
The heat's party gathering
One earth, one place of life
And forever we should be at it's side

One earth my only love
It we should never shun
One earth one planet
Saving it is our main target

Soil Erosion – The Erosion of the Earth

Soil Erosion is the degradation of the soil
Which makes the earth boil
And that leads to global warming
Which is not at all charming

The key to save soil is afforestation
And for this matter there should be no procrastination
This is not a thing to be taken lightly
If you want the future to shine brightly

Right now the Earth is yelling for help loudly
To save the soil which is its glory
It is crucial to save the soil, the root of survival
So that the Earth can return back to normal

Arrogant Corona

Corona, o corona when will you go away ?
Omicron, O omicron why do you make us sway ?
Corona, o corona why are you so cruel ?
Omicron, O omicron why did you stop our school?

Even if you threaten me, I will never go away
And what did I do to make you sway?
Who said I am cruel? I am no reason for your plight!
And did I say don't go to school ? Corona replied

Don't underestimate us ! We will surely curb you !
You have made our cheerful world blue !
Because of your infection we are unable to breathe !
Giving us a dangerous infection is no big feat !

You weaklings ! How will you curb us ?
How did we turn your life upside down?
And of what destruction do you warn ?
Replied the treacherous Omicron.

You will get your reply soon corona !
All of humanity is in our favour
What great thing do you provide ?
Saying this I go inside

I return with a group of friends
To give a fitting reply to who think they are innocent

On our hands we have sanitizers and vaccine
Carrying all this we come out masking

We spray the sanitizer and vaccine on the
overconfident corona
And corona and it's siblings fell to the ground
Into a deep sleep and never to wake up again
And relived us from all our pain

Helpless Earth

The most beautiful planet is the Earth
Come back to your senses and realise it's worth
Join hands together to save the Big Blue Marble
And the Earth will be as fit as a fiddle

The earth always wails for help
As the reckless humans destroy her, she yelps
The Blue Planet has lost its crown
Let's support each other to give back its crown.

Make the Earth Plastic Free

Make the earth plastic free
And the earth will be greener than it can be.
Says the promising voice of hope
Which, in difficult times helps us to cope

The raising voice of the water dwellers
Tell that plastic waste is polluting their waters
The poor calf says, mother ate plastic and is sick,
Due to that she has become so weak

Plastics have been found in the Antarctic
It is uninhabited by humans, and finding plastic
there is so tragic
All these are the warning bells
That to this world we are soon going to bid farewell

Say no to single use plastic
And wait and see the magic
Nature is the earth's only shirt
Please don't cover it with dirt

The True Meaning of Independence

Independence Day is not a mere holiday
It is the day where on the ground the British shackles lay
Spread this message to the future generations
To make saving the country for them an ambition

With your hand on the heart, Tell: Are we really independent?
When women want to raise their voice and are made silent?
When students are not free to follow their dream?
When the politicians enjoy and poor children scream?

Even though we are independent, we are slaves!
Slaves to our money, desires, beliefs and dares!
Are we free from the rich, corrupt politicians?
When they torment with taxes, the poor civilians!

Being constitutionally independent is not enough!
When getting a proper education is tough!
When there are tons of crimes where a million
people suffered,
Tell me, are we really Independent?

It's Your Life

Don't care about what people say
Whether you like or hate the bay
Whether you are short or tall
Or as thin as a stick or as fat as a ball

Even if they say you are stupid
Or your heart is super rigid
Still don't listen to what they say
Just see things in your own way

Don't let other's thoughts impact your mind
Think of yourself as your own guide
Stay positive, be happy
Don't let other's thoughts make you grapy

Dusshera and Krishna Janmasthami

Today is the Birthday of the notorious butter thief,
The incarnation of lord Vishnu came to remove grief
To restore righteousness on the Earth,
On this day, Lord Krishna took birth

Dusshera is the Victory of good over evil
Of good virtues, it is the day of retrieval
Because Lord Rama killed the wicked Ravana
And taught us to follow the middle path, not the extra

Heartfelt Thanks to the Teachers

My heartfelt thanks to all the teachers
Who paint each and every student's life on the canvas
Teachers are the building blocks of the world
To us the theory of life they have unfurled

They release us from the shackles of illiteracy,
They sacrifice their own life to keep us happy
Thank you to all the teachers,
Who taught us manners to make us leaders

Teachers have chiseled us into diamonds
To make us the legends of the future
I thank the teachers from the bottom of my heart
Who have made the world like a piece of art

The Thief

School brings me over the moon,
Whenever I am totally blue
School is the light of my life'
It always stays by my side

But our class has lost its cheer
As the strict teacher it fears
It will be till the thief is caught
And until justice justice is brought

A mad person is writing names on the desks,
And the teacher on us pecks
Funny teachers have turned strict
All jokes, happiness and fun they restrict

We are all shrouded together in fear,
As the petty thief is near
The thief is the lemon in the milk
He is spoiling the reputation of our class's silk

In the end, truth always wins
And the god above is counting our sins
Come thief, get your punishment,
Says god and adds, "The thief will become ancient".

Curb Corruption

Hello people of India, are you all sleeping?
As under corruption we are reeling?
Unpunctual people are eating away our time,
And we have to deal with it for a lifetime!

We earn money with lots of hard work
And to that income taxes play havoc!
If the government takes away half of our money,
Other half in rent, how are we supposed to fill our belly?

Let's raise our voice, for our rights, together
To see a better India in the future
Each and every individual should contribute,
Nothing will be possible if we remain mute !

Earth's Only Shirt

Ozone layer of the earth
Is the earth's only shirt
That shirt protects the Earth like a Bun,
From the harmful rays of the Sun

Sadly the shirt is being damaged
And it doesn't even have a bandage
It happens Due to CFC'S and other chemicals
And that makes us go around in circles

Spread awareness and save a life
And the world will always be on your side
Let's join hands together
To make the Earth beautiful forever

Stupid Questions

I have really stupid questions in my mind
To find the answer, I don't know if the world will
take my side.
How did humans end up like this?
I guess it is the magic of a powerful fist

Why were we chosen to invent a language?
And invent many things like computers and baggage?
How did we develop many things and why did we so much?
It is all magic and only magic, I believe such

We are all fortunate to be chosen like this
It is not just for eternal bliss
God has has entrusted the Earth to us
To make it beautiful, not worse

Koalas

I was teleported to Australia in my dream
Into a forest with a beautiful stream
I saw a teddy like creature in a tree
Munching leaves in a wild glee

A cute koala was the teddy bear
Deforestation is its worst fear
It is a critically endangered animal
Because, the forest to it is magical

Promote afforestation right now!
And the seed of saving the koalas you will sow
Help to stop poaching forever
To help the koalas feel better !

Animal Rights

Animals also have rights to live
They are the world's natives
Why are they tortured in labs,
For testing chemicals and corona jabs?

Why are animals forced to perform in circuses?
Obliviously, it is all just for money and business!
Why do we throw stones at the poor strays?
After all, it is also their place!

Animals are our loving companions
Not just things of attractions
Always be kind to animals
They are our true equals

After All, Home Is Where the Heart Is

Home is where the heart is
Wherever you go, home you always miss
After long trips to beautiful places
The desire to go home always blazes

But many people have nowhere to go
Compassion to these people, we should show
It is surely none of their fault
To bring change in their life, we must revolt

Join hands together to make these people happy
As these people have been affected badly
Give them what they need in a wild glee
And the happiness on their face you will see

Forget and Forgive

Forgiveness is the tool to happiness
Without which we will be steeped in lonliness
Everyone commits grave mistakes
That generates sadness like lakes

Everyone gets angry sometimes
Then soothe yourself with happy rhymes
Always forgive and forget
And tons of happiness everyone will get

Forgive everyone and yourself
Remind everyone of their pure self
The world will be happier than ever
That will be the universe's splendour

My Childhood Memories

Childhood memories are precious things,
Lots of fun and bliss it brings
Which each one of us like to cherish
These memories will never perish

I have many childhood memories
I hope so that you will not tease
I used to eat wheat flour
And my happiness used to be pure

I bathed in ice cream the first time I ate it
And licked and bathed in every single bit
I used to wear my father's t-shirt and roam free
And also his shoes and my mother's sari

I was three when I first played Holi
And used to take teddies for a ride boldly
All these are some of my childhood memories
And they will be with me for centuries

Love for Books

I honestly forever have my nose in my books,
I won't look up even when hung on a thousand hooks!
Much to the annoyance of my parents,
But books give me a world of blissful moments

Whenever I am free, I a snatch a book,
They are magical ones that take me to a brook
Books are forever going to be my life
My best companion and a guide

Read, Read and whenever you can, read
My parents to come and eat plead
Whenever I read books, a new portal opens up
Where I read hiding in a shrub

Books will always be there for me,
Till there is the sun and blue is the sea.
Till there will be mountains and rivers,
Books will erode my mind like beavers

JUST BOOKS!

Irony of Life

Irony is the funniest thing in life
I don't know if you will take my side
A bookshop owner might hate books
Or crooks laugh about crooks

Whenever a man washes his car
Because the rains seem so far
He knows it because he knows the weather
And the next hour, raindrops you can hear

A poet wants to publish his book
But he might hate books
Such is the irony of life
They cut through us like a knife

A messy person might be a cleanliness leader
Whatever you say, irony is a teaser
Irony is beyond our might
Such is the irony of life

Artists are Magicians

Artists are the door to the canvas
They are the living atlas
They create magical places,
Planets, fairies and faces!

Artists beautify the world with strokes
They create landscapes and jokes
They unfurl the hidden side of the world,
Hidden places, gems and pearls

Art is the door to joy
It is not a simple toy
Paint, paint and only paint
And create wonders and giants

Mitali Madhumita

Mitali Madhumita is my inspiration for bravery
The first woman to win the gallantry awards, made history
She saved the lives of nineteen people
And to those she is an Angel

She had been sent to Kabul
And had been living in a hotel
One morning, from the Embassy, she heard a loud bang
And she ran there, 2 km away in a clang

She did not think of her own safety
And set an example of bravery
By jumping under the debris to save people
Amongst the bullets by the people who were evil

She has inspired us to be selfless
Also to be kind, brave and full of freshness
We have to follow her example
And just like her, overcome every hurdle

She will forever reside in our hearts
And she is known in India's every part
Let's all try to be like her
And pass down her bravery to the next year

Tongue Twisters

Accept your challenge to twist your tongue
I hope you won't budge
Aam lai amlai, malai, malai lai aam amlai
Don't cry, fly, be a spy and standby

Tongue twisters are in every language
And are words full of fun in packets
They will surely twist your tongue
Whether you are at home or in a longue

Tempting Cakes

Guess what an integral part of a birthday
Or an anniversary, marriage, or any special day
Undoubtedly it is the cake, a juicy dessert
Which is created by people who are experts

They hold mountains of sweet and fluffy cream
And is the food of every dream
Amidst the cream lie spongy slices full of sugar Syrup
And in our bodies create lots of energy build up

Wait a minute, stop your cakey appetite
If you want your life on your side
Control your sugar intake
And eating cakes a celebration you will make.

Your Uniqueness Is Your Strength

Your uniqueness is your strength
And can help you see the Earth's length
Uniqueness is the best thing
And will get you invisible wings

Every person is undoubtedly unique
And a thing which everyone should seek
Uniqueness never knocks on your door
And says I will come at four

Work hard to achieve uniqueness
And of your life, it will be the canvas
Dig, dig and never give up
And your uniqueness will give a thumbs up

History of Chocolate

Something sweet that melts in your mouth
And produces an aroma appealing to the snout
A smooth, large, brown object which empties your wallet
Yes, I am talking about none other than chocolate

A thing which originated in Mesoamerica
But in a form which is not the present's replica
Cacao beans were ground with millions of helpers
Mixed with cornmeal and chilli peppers

This created a bitter, frothy drink
And was only the royal's drink, just think!
After coming to Europe in 1519, it was used as a medicine
And 1828 came a revolution spin

The chocolate press was invented
And it helped the solid form to be presented
And in the 20th century it was the public's treat
And it soon became a major sweetmeat

Schoolsick

I was schoolsick, not homesick,
As the smog of Covid was thick
As I sat in the home luxury jail
And from the teachers getting tons of mail!

Watching the online classes, I felt bored
I want to go to school, I roared
I felt pangs of School sickness
Which had turned my life into a mess

I Spent days staring out of the window
And obviously feeling low
Waiting for a message that is golden
The message - school is going to reopen

There was only a ray of hope
Just with the situation cope
And await the magical message
Which will be sent by god's grace

Raise Your Voice

Raise your Voice, never be hidden
The idea of change it can thicken
Be fearless, be brave forever
Then you can have the power

Raise your voice, for your rights
For everyone, you will light the lights
You can make the Future bright
And can capture everything in your sight

The Happiest Day

I stood with a frenzy of joy in my heart
Of my life it was the best part
I didn't mind the heavy bag
Which in speed made me lag

It felt like the top of the world
There were the four floors unfurled
A thing which I longed to see since two years
Ever since Covid with us said cheers

I climbed two floors with my bag pack
Seeing things which brought memories back
I walked into one of the many large rooms
And my happiness even more blooms

I was back to my dear school
After two years for which waiting was awful
It was 11th August 2021, a breezy day
Which I spent in abandon gay

Little Sweets

Laddu, peda and kaju barfis
Ras malai, kheer and juicy kulfis
Khaja, rasgulla and jalebis
They can beat other freebies

They are the sweetest and juiciest sweets
their syrupy flavour, when you tongue meets
You will close your eyes in fascination
To eat more you will feel the temptation.

Why and When ?

Why are we the way we are?
Why don't we have the power to see far,
Far, Far away into the future
I hope we can see it sooner

Will trees be the way they are?
Why can't they drive a car?
To escape being cut and made into an art,
Why can't they turn themselves into a cart?

Were flowers the way they are?
Were they just a twinkling star?
Waiting to land on the Earth,
And cover its length and breadth ?

I can't wait to see the days,
When will there be a healthier version of Lays!
Will these things come true ?
I am sure these are due !

Poem by a Bookmark

Bookworms need to rest too,
And I am here to help you.
Engross yourself in the book
But the outside world you should look.

Never give up reading books
To avoid being a crook
Lost in the world of the book
I can never do my job as a cook

Here is a wonderful gem
Who will mark every hem
Of the Marvelous book
Which will fascinate you in a look

Flying Time

How did time pass too quickly,
And has cut though so skilfully!
Eight years of my schooling have passed,
So quickly, that it has quickly become the past!

You will never know that time flies,
And sometimes moves like a tortoise!
I never realised that 2022 will end soon,
And we will be seeing the 2023 moon!

I just realised that I have to enjoy every second,
And step back every time gloom beckoned!
Just follow the mantra to happiness above,
And never burn yourself on the death's stove !

www.ingramcontent.com/pod-product-compliance
Lightning Source LLC
Chambersburg PA
CBHW022030150726
47990CB00002B/891